365 Quotes on Writing That Will Make You a Better Writer

Jerry Payne

Five Boroughs Media & Publishing, LLC

Praise for *365 Quotes on Writing That Will Make You a Better Writer*:

Five Stars! "Jerry Payne has filled a book with some of the best tiny discussions on writing to be found… It would be strange indeed if readers didn't come away at least a little better steeped in the lore of writing."
—*ReaderViews*

"Inspiring, succinct, hard-hitting, and infinitely applicable to the writer's creative soul … there's much to love about the accessibility and invitations packed into *365 Quotes on Writing That Will Make You a Better Writer.*"
—*D. Donovan, Senior Reviewer, Midwest Book Review*

"A gem for writers." Five Stars! "…a treasure trove of insights and a source of constant motivation. Whether you're a seasoned writer or just starting, this collection will undoubtedly enrich your writing and foster a deeper appreciation for the art of writing."
—*Reader's Favorite*

"Jerry Payne's thoughtfully gathered *365 Quotes on Writing That Will Make You a Better Writer* offers inspiration for both the struggling and aspirational author."
—*IndieReader*

365 Quotes on Writing That Will Make You a Better Writer

Jerry Payne

FIRST EDITION

Manufactured in the United States of America

Paperback ISBN: 979-8-9894749-3-6
Hardcover ISBN: 979-8-9894749-4-3

Library of Congress Control Number: 2024925531

Copyright © 2025, Jerry Payne

All Rights Reserved

Five Boroughs Media & Publishing, LLC
info@fiveboroughsbooks.com

How to Read This Book

The 365 quotes in this book offer some of the best writing advice you will ever receive. Within these pages, you'll find insights on the craft of writing, the business of writing, the need to write, the beauty of the written word, the writing process, the traits of successful writers, reasons to write, reasons not to write, the importance of persistence, and countless other invaluable lessons—each a gem in its own right.

The quotes come from writers with names like Dickens, Angelou, Stein, King, Emerson, Sontag, Faulkner, Plath, Didion, Fitzgerald, Eliot, Bradbury, Steinbeck, and Hemingway. You'll also encounter wisdom from lesser-known voices, each with something profound to share about the art of writing.

While certain themes may recur throughout the book, no idea is expressed in the same way twice. Of course not—great writers always speak in ways that are uniquely and inimitably their own.

This is not a book to be devoured in one sitting—or even two or twenty. There are 365 quotes in here for a reason. Your mission is to read one quote each day over the next year and reflect on its meaning. Following each quote, you'll find this author's brief commentary: "My Take." Then, you'll see space provided for you to jot down your thoughts on what the quote means to you. Think before you write. Deeply. Consider how you can put the idea presented in the quote to work for you. How can it make a difference in your writing? Your daily routine? Your career as a writer? What lesson does the quote hold specifically *for you*?

I believe that after a year of engaging with the collective wisdom in this book and applying its lessons, you will have experienced the equivalent of at least several writing workshops—all without leaving home! More importantly, you'll emerge as a better writer: more focused, more inspired, more skilled, and with a deeper understanding and appreciation of your chosen craft.

Have a wonderful year. And as I'm sure the brilliant minds featured in this book would all tell you personally if they could: *keep on writing!*

Jerry Payne
Writer

1.

"There is no greater agony than bearing an untold story inside you."
—Maya Angelou

My take:

Writing is hard, but if you have something to say, not writing is harder!

What it means to you:

_____

_____

_____

_____

_____

2.

"Creativity is a wild mind and a disciplined eye."
—Dorothy Parker

My take:

Lots of people have the former. Fewer have the latter.

What it means to you:

_____

_____

_____

_____

_____

_____

3.

"The best time for planning a book is while you're doing the dishes."

—Agatha Christie

My take:

Hmm...not sure about the dishes but I will admit that inspiration has often hit me in the shower.

What it means to you:

_____

_____

_____

_____

_____

_____

4.

"The difference between the right word and the almost right word is the difference between lightning and a lightning bug."

— Mark Twain

My take:

And sometimes you can just tell, you know? If you write a word and it doesn't feel quite right, grab that Thesaurus. Don't settle for the "almost" right word.

What it means to you:

_____

_____

_____

_____

_____

5.

"We write to taste life twice, in the moment and in retrospect."

—Anaïs Nin

My take:

Right? Writing, especially memoir (my favorite), allows us to relive parts of our life. (Not to mention reexamine those parts.)

What it means to you:

_____

_____

_____

_____

_____

6.

"The first draft is just you telling yourself the story."
—Terry Pratchett

My take:

Yep, that first draft is just for you. Later drafts (sometimes much later drafts) are for your audience.

What it means to you:

_____

_____

_____

_____

_____

7.

"You can make anything by writing."
–C.S. Lewis

My take:

And he should know, right? The Chronicles of Narnia series? The Space Trilogy novels? Clive Staples Lewis could make anything *with his words. How about you?*

What it means to you:

_____

_____

_____

_____

_____

8.

"Writing is the painting of the voice."
—Voltaire

My take:

Writing is a form of art, right? Your words are the brush. Your paper is the canvas.

What it means to you:

_____

_____

_____

_____

_____

9.

"Writing a novel is like driving a car at night. You can see only as far as your headlights, but you can make the whole trip that way."

—E. L. Doctorow

My take:

I've never been one for making detailed outlines. The story will tell you which way it wants to go.

What it means to you:

_____

_____

_____

_____

_____

10.

"Writing is an act of faith, not a trick of grammar."
—E. B. White

My take:

Maybe this is why strict grammarians often don't make great writers...

What it means to you:

_____

_____

_____

_____

_____

_____

11.

"A writer is a world trapped in a person."
—Victor Hugo

My take:

And a book must be the way for that world to get out.

What it means to you:

_____

_____

_____

_____

_____

12.

"There are three rules for writing a novel. Unfortunately, no one knows what they are."
–W. Somerset Maugham

My take:

Ha! Maybe you'll be the one to figure them out.

What it means to you:

_____

_____

_____

_____

_____

_____

13.

"Write drunk, edit sober."
—Ernest Hemingway

My take:

Not sure he meant that literally (although with Papa, who can say?). I think he meant go ahead and write with a lot of creativity and imagination. Take chances. Be bold. Then, go back and reign it all in (if it needs it) during the editing process.

What it means to you:

_____

_____

_____

_____

_____

_____

14.

"Amateurs sit and wait for inspiration, the rest of us just get up and go to work."
—Stephen King

My take:

True. Try treating your book like a job, not a hobby. You'll get a lot more accomplished.

What it means to you:

_____

_____

_____

_____

_____

15.
"You fail only if you stop writing."
—Ray Bradbury

My take:

I've noticed this about a lot of things in life. So don't stop!

What it means to you:

_____

_____

_____

_____

_____

_____

16.

"The purpose of a writer is to keep civilization from destroying itself."
—Albert Camus

My take:

That's a pretty noble purpose if you ask me.

What it means to you:

_____
_____
_____
_____
_____
_____

17.
"Write what should not be forgotten."
—Isabel Allende

My take:

Writing provides permanence. Things, and people, can live on through the written word.

What it means to you:

_____

_____

_____

_____

_____

18.

"Don't tell me the moon is shining; show me the glint of light on broken glass."

—Anton Chekhov

My take:

Every beginning writing course teaches "show, don't tell." This is where that phrase came from.

What it means to you:

_____
_____
_____
_____
_____

19.

"Write without fear. Edit without mercy."
—Unknown

My take:

Maybe this is what Hemingway meant with the drunk/sober quote. The key here is "without mercy." Yeah, you have to be ruthless (but kind).

What it means to you:

_____

_____

_____

_____

_____

_____

20.

"To write is to write is to write is to write is to write is to write is to write is to write."
—Gertrude Stein

My take:

I would have added one more "to write," but that's me.

What it means to you:

_____

_____

_____

_____

_____

_____

21.

"There's no money in poetry, but then there's no poetry in money, either."
—Robert Graves

My take:

Very poetic.

What it means to you:

_____

_____

_____

_____

_____

22.
"*I try to leave out the parts that people skip.*"
—Elmore Leonard

My take:

Oh, that more writers would do this!

What it means to you:

_____

_____

_____

_____

_____

23.

"Writing is a way of talking without being interrupted."
— Jules Renard

My take:

Maybe this is why I like writing more than conversation.

What it means to you:

_____

_____

_____

_____

_____

_____

24.

"You can always edit a bad page. You can't edit a blank page."
—Jodi Picoult

My take:

Another way of saying that you just need to write something down! Fix it later.

What it means to you:

_____

_____

_____

_____

_____

25.

"A writer is someone for whom writing is more difficult than it is for other people."
—Thomas Mann

My take:

Because we care more about gettting it right. Right?

What it means to you:

_____

_____

_____

_____

_____

_____

26.

"The art of writing is the art of discovering what you believe."
—Gustave Flaubert

My take:

The very act of writing often clarifies what's in our heads.

What it means to you:

_____

_____

_____

_____

_____

_____

27.
"The only way to learn to write is to write."
—Red Smith

My take:

This is not to say that classes and workshops and instructional books aren't important. But it's experience that teaches us best.

What it means to you:

_____

_____

_____

_____

_____

_____

28.

"A room without books is like a body without a soul."
—Marcus Tullius Cicero

My take:

Books. They make us human and reveal our humanity.

What it means to you:

_____
_____
_____
_____
_____
_____

29.

"You must write every single day of your life... You must lurk in libraries and climb bookshelves like a spy."

—Ray Bradbury

My take:

You have to be a student of the game!

What it means to you:

_____

_____

_____

_____

_____

30.

"Writing is an exploration. You start from nothing and learn as you go."

—E.L. Doctorow

My take:

And it's a different exploration for each of us. This is one thing that separates the art of writing from other disciplines.

What it means to you:

_____

_____

_____

_____

_____

_____

31.

"Words are, of course, the most powerful drug used by mankind."

—Rudyard Kipling

My take:

Love the way Kipling just sort of threw the "of course" in there. Nice.

What it means to you:

_____

_____

_____

_____

_____

32.

"Writers aren't exactly people... they're a whole bunch of people trying to be one person."

—F. Scott Fitzgerald

My take:

I think this speaks to the writer's (especially the novelist's) need to see the world from different points of view.

What it means to you:

_____

_____

_____

_____

_____

33.

"A writer never has a vacation. For a writer, life consists of either writing or thinking about writing."

—Eugene Ionesco

My take:

I think this is true, although sometimes I wish it were not. I'd love to be able to shut it off sometimes. Hard to do.

What it means to you:

_____

_____

_____

_____

_____

34.

"The secret of getting ahead is getting started."
—Mark Twain

My take:

It's the hardest part, of course. And the most important. Take that step, and you're already ahead of all the wannabe writers.

What it means to you:

_____

_____

_____

_____

_____

_____

35.

"Write hard and clear about what hurts."
–Ernest Hemingway

My take:

"Hard and clear." So very Hemingway.

What it means to you:

_____

_____

_____

_____

_____

_____

36.

"You have to write the book that wants to be written. And if the book will be too difficult for grown-ups, then you write it for children."

—Madeleine L'Engle

My take:

Indeed, what's inside you will tell you what to write. Love the line about "too difficult for grown-ups"!

What it means to you:

_____

_____

_____

_____

_____

37.
"*Writing is its own reward.*"
—Henry Miller

My take:

This is what you tell yourself on those nights when you're wondering how you're going to make the mortgage payment…

What it means to you:

_____

_____

_____

_____

_____

38.

"You don't have to be great to get started, but you have to get started to be great."

—Les Brown

My take:

*In fact, you **won't** be great when you get started. So what? Just get started and see what happens after that.*

What it means to you:

_____

_____

_____

_____

_____

_____

39.

"All good writing is swimming underwater and holding your breath."

—F. Scott Fitzgerald

My take:

I think he's talking about immersion. Taking the plunge. And staying in that space, even if it's uncomfortable.

What it means to you:

_____

_____

_____

_____

_____

_____

40.

"A writer is someone who has written."
—E.L. Doctorow

My take:

You know, maybe it really is this simple. Do you write? Then you're a writer.

What it means to you:

_____

_____

_____

_____

_____

41.

"You can't wait for inspiration. You have to go after it with a club."

–Jack London

My take:

Perhaps a little violently put but definitely the right idea. Jack means you have to find your inspiration and be determined to do so.

What it means to you:

_____

_____

_____

_____

_____

42.

"The only thing that you absolutely have to know, is the way to be quiet."

—William Faulkner

My take:

You can't write without "listening" for the appropriate words.

What it means to you:

_____

_____

_____

_____

_____

43.

"To write well, express yourself like the common people, but think like a wise man."

—Aristotle

My take:

Aristotle knew how to take smart ideas and make them relatable. That's an awesome skill.

What it means to you:

_____

_____

_____

_____

_____

44.

"The hardest part about writing is sitting down to do it."
—Joyce Meyer

My take:

This is a common theme, isn't it? Apparently, it's even a problem for the greats. It's all about getting started. Overcoming procrastination.

What it means to you:

_____

_____

_____

_____

_____

45.

"*I write because I cannot help it.*"
—Charlotte Brontë

My take:

All the greats felt/feel this way. Writing is more than a job. For them, it's a way of life.

What it means to you:

_____

_____

_____

_____

_____

_____

46.

"The most valuable of all talents is that of never using two words when one will do."
—Thomas Jefferson

My take:
Writing concisely is a rare skill, and one you should be honing.

What it means to you:

_____

_____

_____

_____

_____

47.

"The pen is mightier than the sword."
—Edward Bulwer-Lytton

My take:

Eloquent quote. But did you know that it was Bulwer-Lytton who also penned the infamous opening sentence, "It was a dark and stormy night"? Can't be eloquent all the time, I guess...

What it means to you:

_____
_____
_____
_____
_____

48.

"The pen is mightier than the sword if the sword is very short, and the pen is very sharp."

—Terry Pratchett

My take:

A little variation on Bulwer-Lytton's original. I like it.

What it means to you:

_____

_____

_____

_____

_____

49.

"The purpose of writing is not to get published but to help you stay sane."

—Patricia Highsmith

My take:

A good thing to remember when the rejection slips come in or the books don't sell!

What it means to you:

_____

_____

_____

_____

_____

_____

50.

"You don't write because you want to say something, you write because you have something to say."

—F. Scott Fitzgerald

My take:

More writers need to understand this difference. Do you have something to say? Or do you just want to say something?

What it means to you:

_____

_____

_____

_____

_____

51.

"You can't use up creativity. The more you use, the more you have."
—Maya Angelou

My take:

Parents with more than one child often talk about how their love wasn't split when the second was born; it actually doubled. Creativity seems to work a lot like love.

What it means to you:

_____

_____

_____

_____

_____

52.

"The best way to predict the future is to invent it."
—Alan Kay

My take:

And that's what writing can do!

What it means to you:

_____

_____

_____

_____

_____

_____

53.

"Writing is the only thing that, when I do it, I feel like I'm truly alive."
–John Updike

My take:

If you feel like Updike, then you know you're a writer.

What it means to you:

_____
_____
_____
_____
_____

54.

"There are no rules. That is how art is born."
—Helen Frankenthaler

My take:

Helen was a painter but I think her words are just as true for the art of writing.

What it means to you:

_____

_____

_____

_____

_____

55.

"Writing is the only way I have to make sense of the world."
—Michael Ende

My take:

Writing is a tool we can use to describe our world. To our readers, yes, but even (maybe especially) to ourselves.

What it means to you:

_____

_____

_____

_____

_____

56.

"To survive, you must tell stories."

—Umberto Eco

My take:

Well, to survive as a writer, I suppose. But to Eco, life was writing.

What it means to you:

_____

_____

_____

_____

_____

57.

"A word after a word after a word is power."
—Margaret Atwood

My take:

And a word after a word after a word is writing!

What it means to you:

_____

_____

_____

_____

_____

58.

"If there's a book that you want to read, but it hasn't been written yet, then you must write it."

—Toni Morrison

My take:

Sometimes, if you really want something done, you just have to do it yourself.

What it means to you:

_____

_____

_____

_____

_____

_____

59.

"You can fix anything but a blank page."
—Nora Roberts

My take:

That's why writing something that's not so good is better than not writing at all. "Not so good" can become good. Even great. Nothing at all? Well, there's no fix for that.

What it means to you:

_____

_____

_____

_____

_____

60.

"I can shake off everything as I write; my sorrows disappear, my courage is reborn."

—Anne Frank

My take:

And this from someone who knew a little something about sorrows.

What it means to you:

_____

_____

_____

_____

_____

61.

"Fill your paper with the breathings of your heart."
—William Wordsworth

My take:

So much great writing comes from deep within. That's where the good stuff is.

What it means to you:

_____

_____

_____

_____

_____

62.

"Words are a lens to focus one's mind."
—Ayn Rand

My take:

Nothing solidifies an idea like writing it out.

What it means to you:

_____

_____

_____

_____

_____

63.

"The only end of writing is to enable the reader better to enjoy life, or better to endure it."

—Samuel Johnson

My take:

These are two pretty noble goals, if you ask me.

What it means to you:

_____

_____

_____

_____

_____

64.

"You write to communicate to the hearts and minds of others what's burning inside you."
—Arthur Plotnik

My take:

And writing is the only way to put out that fire. Or else to ignite it within another's heart and mind.

What it means to you:

_____

_____

_____

_____

_____

65.

"It is perfectly okay to write garbage—as long as you edit brilliantly."

—C.J. Cherryh

My take:

I suspect a lot of really great writing starts out as garbage. Not many first drafts get published.

What it means to you:

_____

_____

_____

_____

_____

66.

"There are no real rules about writing. Your own rules are the only ones that matter."

—W. Somerset Maugham

My take:

Punctuation, grammar, and spelling matter, but I have a feeling Maugham was talking about style.

What it means to you:

_____

_____

_____

_____

_____

67.

"Writing is a form of therapy; sometimes I wonder how all those who do not write, compose, or paint can manage to escape the madness, melancholia, the panic, and fear which is inherent in a human situation."

—Graham Greene

My take:

I wonder this, too…

What it means to you:

_____

_____

_____

_____

_____

68.

"The purpose of a storyteller is not to tell you how to think, but to give you questions to think upon."

—Brandon Sanderson

My take:

Yes! So many writers want to beat the reader to death with their thoughts. No. Let the reader do the thinking.

What it means to you:

_____

_____

_____

_____

_____

69.

"You must stay drunk on writing so reality cannot destroy you."
—Ray Bradbury

My take:

Reality can sober a person right up. Don't let it do that to you. Beat reality back with your writing!

What it means to you:

_____

_____

_____

_____

_____

_____

70.

"I write to discover what I know."
—Flannery O'Connor

My take:

Because it's already there. Within you. More knowledge than you ever knew was there.

What it means to you:

_____
_____
_____
_____
_____
_____

71.

"The road to hell is paved with adverbs."
—Stephen King

My take:

Those damnable 'ly' words. Get rid of them. Most of the time, they're not needed. "He loudly shouted" works much better as "He shouted." (Is there a quiet way to shout?)

What it means to you:

_____

_____

_____

_____

_____

72.

"A writer is working when he's staring out of the window."
—Burton Rascoe

My take:

This is good to hear. I do a lot of it...

What it means to you:

_____

_____

_____

_____

_____

73.

"A professional writer is an amateur who didn't quit."
—Richard Bach

My take:

That's it. That's the difference.

What it means to you:

_____

_____

_____

_____

_____

74.

"Good writing is like a windowpane."
—George Orwell

My take:

Writing is a conduit, a means by which to see something in a new way. And it should never draw attention to itself. When you're looking through a window, you shouldn't notice the window.

What it means to you:

_____

_____

_____

_____

_____

_____

75.

"The writer must believe that what he is doing is the most important thing in the world. And he must hold to this illusion even when he knows it is not true."

—John Steinbeck

My take:

I think Steinbeck is talking about commitment here. The only way to do one's best is through this kind of commitment.

What it means to you:

_____

_____

_____

_____

_____

76.

"Write what disturbs you, what you fear, what you have not been willing to speak about. Be willing to be split open."
—Natalie Goldberg

My take:

This often takes a lot of courage. But, man, does it make for compelling writing.

What it means to you:

_____

_____

_____

_____

_____

77.

"Writing is a struggle against silence."
—Carlos Fuentes

My take:

Sometimes it would be easier to stay silent about things. Don't stay silent.

What it means to you:

_____

_____

_____

_____

_____

78.

"The secret to creativity is knowing how to hide your sources."

—Albert Einstein

My take:

Ha! Love this. Albert recognized that there's nothing new under the sun. Not really.

What it means to you:

_____

_____

_____

_____

_____

_____

79.
"Writers live twice."
—Natalie Goldberg

My take:
In the "real" world, and in the worlds they create.

What it means to you:

_____

_____

_____

_____

_____

80.

"The art of writing is the art of applying the seat of the pants to the seat of the chair."

—Mary Heaton Vorse

My take:

People often have romantic notions of writers and the writerly life. But most of the time, it's really just this.

What it means to you:

_____

_____

_____

_____

_____

_____

81.

"Easy reading is damn hard writing."
—Nathaniel Hawthorne

My take:

It takes a lot of effort to make it flow easily and sound just right. But it's our job to do the hard work so that it's easy for the reader.

What it means to you:

_____

_____

_____

_____

_____

_____

82.

"If my doctor told me I had only six minutes to live, I wouldn't brood. I'd type a little faster."
—Isaac Asimov

My take:

Now that's commitment!

What it means to you:

_____

_____

_____

_____

_____

83.

"Don't bend; don't water it down; don't try to make it logical; don't edit your own soul according to the fashion. Rather, follow your most intense obsessions mercilessly."

—Franz Kafka

My take:

Be true to your own vision. That's what's going to make your writing genuine and unique!

What it means to you:

_____

_____

_____

_____

_____

84.

"The greatest part of a writer's time is spent in reading in order to write. A man will turn over half a library to make a book."

—Samuel Johnson

My take:

I have always preached this. To write great literature, read great literature.

What it means to you:

_____
_____
_____
_____
_____

85.

"Writing is the geometry of the soul."
—Plato

My take:

Geometry provides structure and order and understanding to shapes, right? Likewise, writing provides structure and order and understanding to our thoughts. Even to who we are.

What it means to you:

_____

_____

_____

_____

_____

_____

86.

"The writer is by nature a dreamer—a conscious dreamer."

—Carson McCullers

My take:

A writer's imagination is not limited to dreams at night. It's alive around the clock.

What it means to you:

_____

_____

_____

_____

_____

87.

"No sentence is so beautiful that it can't be improved."
—Oscar Wilde

My take:

And after that, it can probably be improved again. This is why there's no such thing as perfection in writing.

What it means to you:

_____

_____

_____

_____

_____

88.

"I write to find out what I'm talking about."
—Edward Albee

My take:

What a simple, direct way of putting it. Words clarify our thoughts.

What it means to you:

_____

_____

_____

_____

_____

89.

"Writing is a job, a talent, but it's also the place to go in your head. It is the imaginary friend you drink your tea with in the afternoon."

—Ann Patchett

My take:

Writing makes a wonderful companion.

What it means to you:

_____

_____

_____

_____

_____

90.

"We are all apprentices in a craft where no one ever becomes a master."
—Ernest Hemingway

My take:

This is some statement coming from a master like Hemingway. But Hem understood that the learning never stops.

What it means to you:

_____

_____

_____

_____

_____

91.

"A writer is someone who can make a riddle out of an answer."

—Karl Kraus

My take:

Good writing invites curiosity and deeper thinking. It challenges.

What it means to you:

_____

_____

_____

_____

_____

_____

92.

"The true alchemists do not change lead into gold; they change the world into words."

—William H. Gass

My take:

Thus making writers the true alchemists, making sense of the world through words. Much better than gold.

What it means to you:

_____

_____

_____

_____

_____

_____

93.

"Writing is a way of paying attention."
—Susan Sontag

My take:

Actually, it forces us to pay attention. How else are we going to write if we're not focused on the world around us?

What it means to you:

_____

_____

_____

_____

_____

94.

"To me, the greatest pleasure of writing is not what it's about, but the inner music the words make."

—Truman Capote

My take:

I always recommend reading your work out loud. Does it flow? Does it "make music"?

What it means to you:

_____
_____
_____
_____
_____

95.

"The best style is the style you don't notice."
—Somerset Maugham

My take:

A good writer is like a good umpire. You don't notice unless he makes a bad call. Keep your readers focused on the game: what you're saying, not how you're saying it.

What it means to you:

_____

_____

_____

_____

_____

_____

96.

"There is no real ending. It's just the place where you stop the story."

—Frank Herbert

My take:

Writing, like life, goes on and on.

What it means to you:

_____

_____

_____

_____

_____

_____

97.
"Writing is an act of faith."
—Erica Jong

My take:

We have no idea if what we write is going to land somewhere, if it's going to resonate, if people might like it or get something out of it. But we write anyway…

What it means to you:

_____

_____

_____

_____

_____

98.

"Description begins in the writer's imagination, but should finish in the reader's."
—Stephen King

My take:

Yes! If your reader is fully engaged, their imagination will fill in every detail and flesh out every idea.

What it means to you:

_____
_____
_____
_____
_____
_____

99.

"If a nation loses its storytellers, it loses its childhood."
—Peter Handke

My take:

Life would lose its magic, wouldn't it?

What it means to you:

_____

_____

_____

_____

_____

100.

"Writers are always selling somebody out."
—Joan Didion

My take:

Especially true in nonfiction, isn't it? It's really impossible to sufficiently describe someone so that a reader gets the full picture. Descriptions always seems instead to be subject to the requirements of the story.

What it means to you:

_____

_____

_____

_____

_____

_____

101.

"The wastebasket is a writer's best friend."
—Isaac Bashevis Singer

My take:

Or, today, the "delete" key. All it sometimes takes to correct your writing is to trash it. How simple is that?

What it means to you:

_____

_____

_____

_____

_____

102.

"Start writing, no matter what. The water does not flow until the faucet is turned on."
—Louis L'Amour

My take:

Another way of saying, "Get started!" I do hope you're heeding this advice.

What it means to you:

_____

_____

_____

_____

_____

_____

103.

"You should write because you love the shape of stories and sentences and the creation of different words on a page."

—Annie Proulx

My take:

That's why writers write. Why are you writing? Be honest.

What it means to you:

_____

_____

_____

_____

_____

104.

"There are no laws for the novel. There never have been, nor can there ever be."
–Doris Lessing

My take:

Ever wonder where the word "novel" came from? How can anything ever be "novel" if it's hemmed in by rules?

What it means to you:

_____

_____

_____

_____

_____

_____

105.

"Inspiration is a guest that does not willingly visit the lazy."

–Pyotr Tchaikovsky

My take:

I can say from experience that the harder I work, the more "inspired" I become.

What it means to you:

_____

_____

_____

_____

_____

106.

"The worst enemy to creativity is self-doubt."
—Sylvia Plath

My take:

Self-doubt is always saying, "That will never work." But everybody has self-doubts. Everybody. Find your way around them.

What it means to you:

_____

_____

_____

_____

_____

107.

"Creativity is allowing yourself to make mistakes. Art is knowing which ones to keep."
—Scott Adams

My take:

And, by extension, which ones to toss.

What it means to you:

_____

_____

_____

_____

_____

108.

"Don't try to figure out what other people want to hear from you; figure out what you have to say. It's the one and only thing you have to offer."

—Barbara Kingsolver

My take:

It's a common mistake to try to guess what the audience wants to read. Forget all that. Write what you want (or need) to write.

What it means to you:

_____

_____

_____

_____

_____

109.

"The characters that I create are ones that I know well. And when I'm writing, I try to follow them instead of making them follow me."

—Haruki Murakami

My take:

Listen to your characters. If you've fleshed them out sufficiently, they'll tell you where to take them.

What it means to you:

_____

_____

_____

_____

_____

110.

"To produce a mighty book, you must choose a mighty theme."

—Herman Melville

My take:

And Melville was a writer who knew a thing about mighty books and mighty themes. (Not to mention mighty whales...)

What it means to you:

_____

_____

_____

_____

_____

_____

111.

"The best stories don't come from 'good vs. bad' but 'good vs. good'."
—Leo Tolstoy

My take:

And this is so because the complexity of the human psyche is endlessly fascinating.

What it means to you:

_____

_____

_____

_____

_____

_____

112.

"The most powerful words in English are 'Tell me a story.'"
—Pat Conroy

My take:

It's innate, isn't it? It shouldn't be surprising that children say this almost as soon as they can talk.

What it means to you:

_____

_____

_____

_____

_____

113.

"The role of a writer is not to say what we all can say, but what we are unable to say."

—Anaïs Nin

My take:

Writers put our thoughts into words, even (maybe especially) the ones we don't want to say out loud.

What it means to you:

_____

_____

_____

_____

_____

_____

114.

"When writing a novel a writer should create living people; people, not characters. A character is a caricature."

—Ernest Hemingway

My take:

Ever read a novel where all the characters seemed cliched? Pretty boring wasn't it? Don't let that happen to your characters.

What it means to you:

_____

_____

_____

_____

_____

_____

115.

"A story has to have a beginning, a middle, and an end, but not necessarily in that order."

–Jean-Luc Godard

My take:

Ooh, I like this. Another way of reminding you that there are no rules. You're limited by your imagination!

What it means to you:

_____

_____

_____

_____

_____

_____

116.

"Half my life is an act of revision."
–John Irving

My take:

I think we're all a little like this, no? Doing, learning, making changes, relearning. Hmm...seems like the process of writing is a lot like the process of living.

What it means to you:

_____

_____

_____

_____

_____

117.

"Words can be like X-rays if you use them properly—they'll go through anything. You read and you're pierced."

—Aldous Huxley

My take:

Well, the right words, that is. Yes, good writing heads straight for the heart.

What it means to you:

_____

_____

_____

_____

_____

118.

"The scariest moment is always just before you start."
—Stephen King

My take:

And this from a guy who knows a thing or two about scary moments...

What it means to you:

_____
_____
_____
_____
_____

119.

"A word is dead when it is said, some say. I say it just begins to live that day."
—Emily Dickinson

My take:

Emily disagrees with the idea that once something is spoken it loses its mystery or potency. For her, the word's life now begins in the mind of the reader. I'm with her.

What it means to you:

_____

_____

_____

_____

_____

120.

"Any (person) who keeps working is not a failure. He may not be a great writer, but he'll eventually make some kind of career for himself as a writer."

—Ray Bradbury

My take:

Great practical advice. Nothing beats good old-fashioned hard work.

What it means to you:

_____

_____

_____

_____

_____

121.

"Creativity takes courage."
—Henri Matisse

My take:

Why? Because creativity means producing something new. And that means putting yourself out there. You have to have courage to do that.

What it means to you:

_____

_____

_____

_____

_____

122.

"The hardest thing about writing is writing."
—Nora Ephron

My take:

Yes, the actual act! The sitting down and doing.

What it means to you:

_____

_____

_____

_____

_____

123.

"Your style is the intersection of what you love and what you know."

–Zadie Smith

My take:

And that point will always be completely you, *which is what makes your style unique.*

What it means to you:

124.

"The profession of book writing makes horse racing seem like a solid, stable business."

—John Steinbeck

My take:

Yep, that seems about right.

What it means to you:

_____

_____

_____

_____

_____

125.

"The task of a writer consists of being able to make something out of an idea."
–Thomas Mann

My take:

Ideas are nebulous and strictly conceptual until someone comes along and puts them into words.

What it means to you:

_____

_____

_____

_____

_____

_____

126.

"The creative adult is the child who survived."
—Ursula K. Le Guin

My take:

Who's more creative and imaginative than a child? Don't ever lose that, no matter how old you get.

What it means to you:

_____
_____
_____
_____
_____

127.

"The writer's curse is that even in solitude, no matter its duration, he never grows lonely or bored."

—Criss Jami

My take:

Hmm...what do you think? Curse? Or Blessing?

What it means to you:

_____

_____

_____

_____

_____

128.

"Writing is the only profession where no one considers you ridiculous if you earn no money."

—Jules Renard

My take:

Good thing, huh?

What it means to you:

_____

_____

_____

_____

_____

129.

"Every writer I know has trouble writing."
–Joseph Heller

My take:

I find this very encouraging. It's not easy, right? We think it must be easy for the greats but it isn't.

What it means to you:

_____

_____

_____

_____

_____

130.

"Most of the basic material a writer works with is acquired before the age of fifteen."
—Willa Cather

My take:

I think she's talking about our personalities, worldviews, and the unique ways we each express ourselves. Even our love of the written word. This is the material we work with, and it's built early on.

What it means to you:

_____

_____

_____

_____

_____

131.

"One day I will find the right words, and they all will be simple."

–Jack Kerouac

My take:

Hemingway could have said this, too. Yes, the right words are almost always simple ones.

What it means to you:

_____

_____

_____

_____

_____

132.

"Creativity is contagious. Pass it on."
—Albert Einstein

My take:

This is why it's important to keep writing. You never know whom you might inspire with your words.

What it means to you:

_____

_____

_____

_____

_____

_____

133.

"A blank piece of paper is God's way of telling us how hard it is to be God."
—Sidney Sheldon

My take:

Creating a world from scratch. Not easy. But that's what every book requires.

What it means to you:

_____

_____

_____

_____

_____

134.

"The writer is an explorer. Every step is an advance into a new land."

—Ralph Waldo Emerson

My take:

And not just any land. A land that you create!

What it means to you:

_____

_____

_____

_____

_____

_____

135.

"I write entirely to find out what I'm thinking, what I'm looking at, what I see and what it means."

—Joan Didion

My take:

In fact, sometimes you don't have any idea what you think of something until you write it out.

What it means to you:

_____

_____

_____

_____

_____

_____

136.

"Creativity is the sudden cessation of stupidity."
—Edwin Land

My take:

Creativity requires you to transcend the ordinary, vapid, inane thoughts. Creativity is intelligence.

What it means to you:

_____
_____
_____
_____
_____
_____

137.

"Writing is a socially acceptable form of schizophrenia."
—E.L. Doctorow

My take:

Are you a fiction writer? Then you know that you can't write an effective character without getting into that character's head. Without being that character.

What it means to you:

_____

_____

_____

_____

_____

138.

"It is only by writing, not dreaming about it, that we develop our own style."
—P.D. James

My take:

Oh, this is so true. Beginning writers obssess over their "style." Your style will present itself organically. Just keep writing!

What it means to you:

_____

_____

_____

_____

_____

139.

"If you don't have time to read, you don't have the time (or the tools) to write. Simple as that."

—Stephen King

My take:

I've said it before and I'll say it again: To write great literature, read great literature.

What it means to you:

_____

_____

_____

_____

_____

_____

140.

"You never have to change anything you got up in the middle of the night to write."
—Saul Bellow

My take:

I've never been a middle-of-the-night writer, but I think what Bellow means is that if you're inspired enough by an idea to get out of bed to write it, it's probably a pretty good idea.

What it means to you:

_____

_____

_____

_____

_____

141.

"The road to hell is paved with works-in-progress."
—Philip Roth

My take:

Stephen King said the road to hell is paved with adverbs. I suppose for writers there may be more than one road!

What it means to you:

_____

_____

_____

_____

_____

142.

"Start before you're ready."
—Steven Pressfield

My take:

If you wait until you're sure you're "ready," you'll probably be waiting a long, long time.

What it means to you:

_____
_____
_____
_____
_____

143.

"The difference between fiction and reality? Fiction has to make sense."
—Tom Clancy

My take:

Ha! How true. We'll put up with a lot of nonsensical stuff in real life, but if that novel we're reading is illogical, that's a deal-killer.

What it means to you:

_____

_____

_____

_____

_____

144.

"I went for years not finishing anything. Because, of course, when you finish something you can be judged."

—Erica Jong

My take:

I think this stops a lot of people. Don't let it stop you.

What it means to you:

_____

_____

_____

_____

_____

145.

"Writing comes more easily if you have something to say."
—Sholem Asch

My take:
If you're ever really blocked, ask yourself what it is you're trying to say.

What it means to you:

_____

_____

_____

_____

_____

146.

"There is no greater joy than to compose a story and then rest your head in peace, knowing you've said what you've always wanted to say."

—George R.R. Martin

My take:

Indeed. Nothing is more satisfying. (And I'm including ice cream here.)

What it means to you:

_____

_____

_____

_____

_____

147.

"Writing means sharing. It's part of the human condition to want to share things – thoughts, ideas, opinions."
—Paulo Coelho

My take:

Knowing others will be reading is a big part of my motivation. (I don't know how Emily Dickinson did it. She wrote her poems and stuffed them in a drawer.)

What it means to you:

_____
_____
_____
_____
_____

148.

"The pages are still blank, but there is a miraculous feeling of the words being there, written in invisible ink and clamoring to become visible."
—Vladimir Nabokov

My take:

Kind of like the idea that there's a work of sculptured art inside a block of stone, just waiting to be released.

What it means to you:

_____

_____

_____

_____

_____

149.

"Creativity is an act of defiance."
—Twyla Tharp

My take:

And this is because creativity conjurs up something new, and new things always challenge the status quo.

What it means to you:

_____

_____

_____

_____

_____

150.

"Writing is an occupation in which you have to keep proving your talent to people who have none."

—Jules Renard

My take:

And isn't it those talentless people who are always the first to criticize?

What it means to you:

_____
_____
_____
_____
_____
_____

151.

"I am a drinker with writing problems."

—Brendan Behan

My take:
A man after my own heart…

What it means to you:

_____

_____

_____

_____

_____

152.

"A short story is a love affair, a novel is a marriage."
—Lorrie Moore

My take:

And with everything a marriage entails. All the ups and downs of the long-haul.

What it means to you:

_____

_____

_____

_____

_____

153.

"Writing is a kind of revenge against reality."
—Mario Vargas Llosa

My take:

Maybe the best revenge. Want to get back at reality? Write one that obeys your rules.

What it means to you:

_____

_____

_____

_____

_____

154.

"One always has a better book in one's mind than one can manage to get onto paper."
—Michael Cunningham

My take:

I think this is true. The idea in one's head is rarely captured in print. But that's no reason not to try.

What it means to you:

_____

_____

_____

_____

_____

155.

"Each writer is born with a repertory company in his head."

—Gore Vidal

My take:

And they're all at your disposal 24 hours a day. How cool is that?

What it means to you:

156.

"Writing well means never having to say, 'I guess you had to be there.'"

—Jef Mallett

My take:

And that's because if you've done it right, you've taken the reader "there."

What it means to you:

_____

_____

_____

_____

_____

157.

> "Sometimes a writer has to remind the reader of the point of the story. Other times, he has to remind himself."
>
> —Gene Wolfe

My take:

Ever find yourself stopping and saying, "Wait—now what was my point again?" I know I have!

What it means to you:

_____

_____

_____

_____

_____

158.

"Good books don't give up all their secrets at once."
—Stephen King

My take:

I am constantly telling my memoir clients this. They want to get everything out in the first chapter. Give the reader a reason to keep reading!

What it means to you:

_____

_____

_____

_____

_____

159.

"If I waited for perfection, I would never write a word."
—Margaret Atwood

My take:

I think this is where a lot of people get stuck. You have to know that it's never going to be perfect. Do it anyway.

What it means to you:

_____

_____

_____

_____

_____

160.

"The best way to have a good idea is to have a lot of ideas."
—Linus Pauling

My take:

True, because a lot of your ideas just aren't going to pan out. But keep 'em coming. One of them surely will.

What it means to you:

_____
_____
_____
_____
_____

161.

"Writers don't write from experience. If you did, you'd get maybe one book, maybe three poems. Writers write from empathy."
—Nikki Giovanni

My take:

And empathy is universal. You don't need to have lived a character's life to know what that character feels.

What it means to you:

_____

_____

_____

_____

_____

_____

162.

"When it is bad, nothing is as bad as writing."
—Ernest Hemingway

My take:

Hem was right. Some things can still work even if they're done poorly. Writing is not one of those things.

What it means to you:

_____

_____

_____

_____

_____

163.

"When in doubt, have a man come through a door with a gun in his hand."
—Raymond Chandler

My take:

Great advice from the best detective novelist ever. (Not sure it works with every genre, however...)

What it means to you:

_____

_____

_____

_____

_____

164.

"Don't be a writer; be writing."
—William Faulkner

My take:

I think a lot of people get caught up in the idea of being "a writer." They just sort of forget to, you know, write!

What it means to you:

_____

_____

_____

_____

_____

165.

"*I want to write books that unlock the traffic jam in everybody's head.*"
–John Updike

My take:

A good story or novel or essay does this, right? It clarifies an idea, or ideas, for the reader. It get them thinking. It gets them moving again. It takes them off dead-center.

What it means to you:

_____

_____

_____

_____

_____

166.

"Your intuition knows what to write, so get out of the way."
—Ray Bradbury

My take:

Don't overthink it! I wonder how many great ideas were stopped in their tracks because the writer didn't listen to their gut.

What it means to you:

_____

_____

_____

_____

_____

167.

"The way to write is to throw your body at the mark when your arrows are spent."
—Ralph Waldo Emerson

My take:

I think Emerson means that sometimes you have to dig down deep and find that motivation, even when you're out of ideas and all of your skill and technique can seemingly take you no further.

What it means to you:

_____

_____

_____

_____

_____

168.

"If you don't turn your life into a story, you just become a part of someone else's story."
—Terry Pratchett

My take:

Are you the main character in your life, or an extra?

What it means to you:

_____

_____

_____

_____

_____

169.

"Good writing is often about letting go of fear and affectation."
—Stephen King

My take:

This affectation thing is huge. Writing that is artificial and designed to impress? Readers see right through it.

What it means to you:

_____

_____

_____

_____

_____

170.

"No tears in the writer, no tears in the reader."
—Robert Frost

My take:

If you're not feeling it, how can you possibly expect your readers to feel it?

What it means to you:

_____

_____

_____

_____

_____

_____

171.

"Read, read, read. Read everything—trash, classics, good and bad, and see how they do it. Just like a carpenter who works as an apprentice and studies the master."

—William Faulkner

My take:

Now this is interesting. I am always advising writers to read great literature. Faulkner is saying there is even value in reading "trash." Maybe so?

What it means to you:

_____

_____

_____

_____

_____

172.

"Perfectionism is the voice of the oppressor."
—Anne Lamott

My take:

And you have to escape it. Or it will hold you and keep you down.

What it means to you:

_____

_____

_____

_____

_____

173.

"The hard part about writing a novel is finishing it."
—Ernest Hemingway

My take:

This, in contrast to the other perceived "hard part"—getting started! Hmm…maybe it's a tie.

What it means to you:

_____

_____

_____

_____

_____

174.

"Substitute 'damn' every time you're inclined to write 'very'; your editor will delete it and the writing will be just as it should be."

—Mark Twain

My take:

I'm not sure this would work nowadays (what editor would delete "damn"?), but the sentiment sure holds up.

What it means to you:

_____

_____

_____

_____

_____

175.

"An exclamation point is like laughing at your own joke."
—F. Scott Fitzgerald

My take:

They're okay in dialogue, but if you feel the need to use an exclamation point to clue the reader in on the importance of the sentence, then you need to rewrite the sentence. Use words to tell the story, not punctuation marks.

What it means to you:

_____

_____

_____

_____

_____

176.

"Always be a poet, even in prose."
—Charles Baudelaire

My take:

In fact, I recommend reading and writing poetry as exercises to become better at writing prose. Poetry requires total commitment to choosing the exact right words. Good habit to get into.

What it means to you:

_____

_____

_____

_____

_____

_____

177.

"Your voice is your voice. It was the first thing you ever used when you made sounds to your mother. Your voice is your personality."

—Tom Wolfe

My take:

Which is why you should never try to imitate.

What it means to you:

_____

_____

_____

_____

_____

178.

"Don't overwrite. Take out two-thirds of the adjectives and adverbs in your first draft."
—John Dos Passos

My take:

Love this. And yes, it's true. You can actually make your writing better by **eliminating** *words.*

What it means to you:

_____
_____
_____
_____
_____
_____

179.

"A good writer possesses not only his own spirit but also the spirit of his friends."

—Friedrich Nietzsche

My take:

I think Nietzsche is referring to how your writing should be informed by, and relatable to, others.

What it means to you:

_____

_____

_____

_____

_____

_____

180.

"Only those who will risk going too far can possibly find out how far one can go."

—T.S. Eliot

My take:

You never know until you try, right?

What it means to you:

_____

_____

_____

_____

_____

_____

181.

"I always write a good first line, but I have trouble in writing the others."
—Molière

My take:

Well, the first line is important. Problem is, the ones that follow are, too.

What it means to you:

_____

_____

_____

_____

_____

_____

182.

"The more you leave out, the more you highlight what you leave in."
—Henry Green

My take:

Addition by subtraction. The famous "theory of omission."

What it means to you:

_____

_____

_____

_____

_____

183.

"If it sounds like writing, I rewrite it."
—Elmore Leonard

My take:

Ever read anything that makes you think the writer was simply trying too hard? Don't be that writer.

What it means to you:

_____

_____

_____

_____

_____

184.

"It's not the first draft that's the hardest, it's what you do with it afterward."
—Douglas Adams

My take:

The first draft isn't necessarily easy, but the real work comes with turning it into its absolute best version.

What it means to you:

_____
_____
_____
_____
_____
_____

185.

"A short story is a different thing all together – a short story is like a kiss in the dark from a stranger."

—Stephen King

My take:

Great short stories are immediate, impactful, and intriguing.

What it means to you:

_____

_____

_____

_____

_____

186.

"Writer's block is a fancy term made up by whiners so they can have an excuse to drink alcohol."
—Steve Martin

My take:

Ha! I think he might be right. Don't allow writer's block to be your excuse for anything.

What it means to you:

_____

_____

_____

_____

_____

187.

"The best way out is always through."
—Robert Frost

My take:

When you get stuck, there's only one direction to take: straight ahead (and this from a guy who wrote about forks in the road…)

What it means to you:

_____

_____

_____

_____

_____

188.

"I write when I'm inspired, and I see to it that I'm inspired at nine o'clock every morning."

—Peter De Vries

My take:

Make writing a routine. Treat it not like a hobby, but like the serious pursuit that it is

What it means to you:

_____

_____

_____

_____

_____

189.

"Ideas are like rabbits. You get a couple and learn how to handle them, and pretty soon you have a dozen."

–John Steinbeck

My take:

Indeed. Colorful way of saying that creativity begets more creativity.

What it means to you:

_____

_____

_____

_____

_____

190.

"Writing a novel is like making love, but it's also like having a tooth pulled. Pleasure and pain. Sometimes it's like making love while having a tooth pulled."

—Dean Koontz

My take:

Yep, writing runs the gamut.

What it means to you:

_____

_____

_____

_____

_____

191.

"I hate writing, I love having written."
—Dorothy Parker

My take:

Not sure I totally share this sentiment, but there's no doubt that it's a satisfying feeling to have completed a book or a story or an essay.

What it means to you:

_____

_____

_____

_____

_____

192.

"I love deadlines. I like the whooshing sound they make as they fly by."
—Douglas Adams

My take:

Putting me in mind of a college friend who would often say about his drinking, "I know my limit; I say, 'Hi, Limit. Bye, Limit!'"

What it means to you:

_____

_____

_____

_____

_____

193.

"We have to continually be jumping off cliffs and developing our wings on the way down."

—Kurt Vonnegut

My take:

Take risks. Learn from them.

What it means to you:

_____

_____

_____

_____

_____

_____

194.

"When people tell you something doesn't work for them, they are almost always right. When they tell you how to fix it, they are almost always wrong."

—Neil Gaiman

My take:

So true. Keep it in mind when you have friends read your work.

What it means to you:

_____

_____

_____

_____

_____

_____

195.

"*I try to create sympathy for my characters, then turn the monsters loose.*"
—Stephen King

My take:

You can't expect your readers to become seriously involved unless they can relate to your characters.

What it means to you:

_____

_____

_____

_____

_____

_____

196.

"A wounded deer leaps the highest."
—Emily Dickinson

My take:

Some of our best inspiration comes from some of the worst moments of our lives. (Leave it to Emily to put it so poetically.)

What it means to you:

_____
_____
_____
_____
_____
_____

197.

"Creativity is the power to connect the seemingly unconnected."
—William Plomer

My take:

The ability to see possibilities in relationships and concepts that nobody else has seen is the key to innovation.

What it means to you:

_____

_____

_____

_____

_____

198.

"The creative process is a process of surrender, not control."
–Julia Cameron

My take:

Creativity doesn't work for you. As a writer, you work for Creativity.

What it means to you:

_____

_____

_____

_____

_____

199.

"Every artist was first an amateur."

—Ralph Waldo Emerson

My take:

Even Shakespeare started out as an inexperienced hack. If you're not feeling it, do not get discouraged. It'll come.

What it means to you:

_____

_____

_____

_____

_____

_____

200.

"The principle of true art is not to portray, but to evoke."
—Jerzy Kosinski

My take:

Are you writing things that are going to get people thinking? Or feeling something? Are you moving them? Touching them? Making them laugh or cry? If so, then you're producing art.

What it means to you:

_____

_____

_____

_____

_____

201.

"If writing seems hard, it's because it is hard. It's one of the hardest things people do."
—William Zinsser

My take:

In other words, it's not just you! We all feel that way.

What it means to you:

_____

_____

_____

_____

_____

202.

"Fiction reveals truth that reality obscures."
—Jessamyn West

My take:

Is fiction in some way more honest than nonfiction? Seems counterintuitive, but I think West might be right.

What it means to you:

_____
_____
_____
_____
_____
_____

203.

"Lower your standards and keep writing."
—William Stafford

My take:

Another way of reminding you to forget perfection. Get it down. Fix it later.

What it means to you:

_____

_____

_____

_____

_____

_____

204.

"Write a little every day, without hope, without despair."

—Karen Blixen

My take:

Forget how you feel about it. Just write a little. Every day.

What it means to you:

_____

_____

_____

_____

_____

205.

"You don't always have to write the story. Sometimes you just need to let it write you."
—Dani Shapiro

My take:

Let the story go where it must!

What it means to you:

_____

_____

_____

_____

_____

206.

"Begin anywhere."
—John Cage

My take:

I had a client once who really struggled to begin each chapter. Finally, I told her to forget the first paragraph of the chapter. Start with the second. Then keep writing. Later, circle back to the beginning of the chapter to figure out how to start it. It worked!

What it means to you:

_____

_____

_____

_____

_____

207.

"The desire to write grows with writing."
—Erasmus

My take:

I know this from experience. The more you do it, the more you want to do it. After a while, it doesn't seem like work anymore.

What it means to you:

_____

_____

_____

_____

_____

_____

208.

"Throw up into your typewriter every morning. Clean up every noon."
—Raymond Chandler

My take:

Let's hope Chandler didn't mean this literally! I think he meant just focus on getting something down on paper. Then, edit.

What it means to you:

_____

_____

_____

_____

_____

209.

"Inspiration is everywhere; the key is noticing."
—Stephen Nachmanovitch

My take:

Maybe you'll find inspiration in a song. In a sunrise. In your child's laughter. Pay attention to the world around you. It's all right there in front of you.

What it means to you:

_____

_____

_____

_____

_____

210.

"Write about what you can't forget."
—Mary Karr

My take:

If you can't forget it, it must be powerful in some way. Maybe in a good way; maybe in a bad way. Either way, if you can make your reader feel that power, you'll have a great piece of writing.

What it means to you:

_____
_____
_____
_____
_____

211.

"The greatest thing a writer can do is make people feel."
—Ernest J. Gaines

My take:

It's good to make people think. It's better to make them feel.

What it means to you:

_____

_____

_____

_____

_____

212.

"Clarity is the key to good writing. If it's not clear, it's not communication."

—James Thurber

My take:

We sometimes forget in all the talk about plot and characters and being creative that at its most basic, writing is about communication, about having your reader understand you.

What it means to you:

_____

_____

_____

_____

_____

213.

"Style is knowing who you are, what you want to say, and not giving a damn."
—Gore Vidal

My take:

Being yourself, in other words.

What it means to you:

_____

_____

_____

_____

_____

_____

214.

"Brevity is the soul of wit." —William Shakespeare

My take:

An oldie but a goodie. Keep it streamlined.

What it means to you:

_____

_____

_____

_____

_____

215.

"If you're not willing to revise, you're not really willing to write."

—Nigel Watts

My take:

Because writing is rewriting. You can't stop at the first draft and think you've written. You've only drafted.

What it means to you:

_____

_____

_____

_____

_____

216.

"Read your work aloud. The ear catches what the eye misses."

—Truman Capote

My take:

I love this advice. Reading aloud lets you hear the flow of the words. How does it sound?

What it means to you:

_____

_____

_____

_____

_____

_____

217.

"Find your voice and hone it until it's unmistakable."
—Margaret Atwood

My take:
I find this happens naturally if you just keep at it.

What it means to you:

_____

_____

_____

_____

_____

218.
"Simplify, simplify."
—Henry David Thoreau

My take:

Another oldie but goodie. How much potentially great work, I wonder, is marred by overly complex writing?

What it means to you:

_____

_____

_____

_____

_____

219.

"Good writing makes the reader forget they're reading."
—Paul Bowles

My take:

Instead, it just becomes an enjoyable, captivating, enthralling experience.

What it means to you:

_____
_____
_____
_____
_____

220.

"Ideas are cheap. It's the execution that is all-important."
—George R.R. Martin

My take:

There is truth to this. The best writers can take seemingly mundane ideas and turn them into something special.

What it means to you:

_____

_____

_____

_____

_____

221.

"Writing is easy. All you have to do is cross out the wrong words."
—Mark Twain

My take:

Simple, right?

What it means to you:

_____

_____

_____

_____

_____

222.

"Sometimes you just have to put down your pen and dig out a typewriter."
—Elizabeth Hay

My take:

Or, nowadays, your computer. What does she mean? She means that eventually you have to stop thinking about it and just write it.

What it means to you:

_____

_____

_____

_____

_____

223.

"The best stories come to you, not when you chase them, but when you are still enough to listen."

—Aimee Bender

My take:

Find a way to quiet the noise in your head and listen for the ideas that are there just waiting to be discovered.

What it means to you:

_____

_____

_____

_____

_____

224.

"Don't plan it all. Let life surprise you, and write about the surprise."
—Julia Cameron

My take:

It's tempting to try to script everything, isn't it? But the beauty of life is often in the unscripted. So it is with writing.

What it means to you:

_____

_____

_____

_____

_____

225.

> "Write the story that scares you, that makes you feel uncertain, that isn't comfortable. I dare you."
> —Cheryl Strayed

My take:

And I triple-dog dare you.

What it means to you:

_____

_____

_____

_____

_____

226.

"A book is a heart that only beats in the chest of another."
—Rebecca Solnit

My take:

A book comes alive only when someone engages with it.

What it means to you:

_____

_____

_____

_____

_____

_____

227.

"I write to give myself strength. I write to be the characters that I am not. I write to explore all the things I'm afraid of."

—Joss Whedon

My take:

I think a lot of writers do this. In writing, we can be anything we want to be.

What it means to you:

_____
_____
_____
_____
_____

228.

"Each time someone dies, a library burns."
—Jandy Nelson

My take:

Don't take your ideas and your knowledge with you. Write that book!

What it means to you:

_____

_____

_____

_____

_____

_____

229.

"Writing is easy. All you do is sit down at a typewriter and open a vein."
—Red Smith

My take:

Yep, that's all it takes...

What it means to you:

_____

_____

_____

_____

_____

230.

"We do not write in order to be understood. We write in order to understand."
—Cecil Day-Lewis

My take:

Maybe my favorite quote about writing. All writing is an exploration. What will you come to understand by writing?

What it means to you:

_____

_____

_____

_____

_____

_____

231.

"A book is simply the container of an idea—like a bottle."

—Angela Carter

My take:

The theme—always remember your theme. That's what your book should be carrying.

What it means to you:

_____

_____

_____

_____

_____

232.

"The theme connects you to the reader somewhere beyond both of you, in that shared space where we all experience the timeless truths of what it means to be human."

—Jerry Payne

My take:

Hey, it's my book. I can put in a quote of my own if I want to!

What it means to you:

_____

_____

_____

_____

_____

233.

"Outlining is like putting on training wheels. It gives me the courage to write, but we always go off the outline."

—Hallie Ephron

My take:

An outline certainly does provide a level of security, like a map or a set of instructions that we can lean on. But Hallie is right. Don't expect it to remain constant.

What it means to you:

_____
_____
_____
_____
_____

234.

"I think I did pretty well, considering I started out with nothing but a bunch of blank paper."

—Steve Martin

My take:

Hey, sometimes you just have to give yourself permission to feel good about any *efforts you make!*

What it means to you:

_____

_____

_____

_____

_____

235.

"Make them laugh, make them cry, but most of all, make them wait."

—Charles Dickens.

My take:

Don't let your story unfold too quickly! Keep the reader on their toes and give them just enough to keep them reading.

What it means to you:

_____

_____

_____

_____

_____

236.

"The power of saying 'People worth talking' to instead of 'People with whom it is worthwhile to talk' is not one to be lightly surrendered."

—H.W. Fowler

My take:

People often get hung up on grammatical "rules" that should never take precedence over flow.

What it means to you:

_____

_____

_____

_____

_____

237.

"Every sentence must do one of two things—reveal character or advance the action."

—Kurt Vonnegut

My take:

Vonnegut really simplifies it here, doesn't he? And he's absolutely right. Everything else is superfluous.

What it means to you:

_____
_____
_____
_____
_____

238.

"The stories that you tell yourself are the ones that matter most."
–Jeanne Moreau

My take:

Be mindful of your inner dialogue. Self-perception is a powerful force on one's reality.

What it means to you:

_____

_____

_____

_____

_____

_____

239.

"The universe is made of stories, not atoms." —Muriel Rukeyser

My take:

And feelings and emotions and experiences. Not things.

What it means to you:

_____

_____

_____

_____

_____

_____

240.

"A writer is a professional eavesdropper."
—Mary Oliver

My take:

The best writers are always paying attention to what's around them, always studying people and the world.

What it means to you:

_____
_____
_____
_____
_____

241.

"Don't be afraid to cut. It's better to have a short, powerful piece than a long, weak one."

—Katherine Mansfield

My take:

Universally true.

What it means to you:

_____

_____

_____

_____

_____

242.

"Characters are not created by writers. They pre-exist and have to be found."
—Elizabeth Bowen

My take:

That means it's up to you to find just the right characters for your work.

What it means to you:

_____

_____

_____

_____

_____

243.

"The story must strike a nerve in me. My heart should start pounding when I hear the first line in my head."
—Susan Sontag

My take:

Do you feel that way about the story you're about to start writing? If not, why not?

What it means to you:

_____
_____
_____
_____
_____

244.

"If the book is true, it will find an audience that is meant to read it."

—Wally Lamb

My take:

Lamb doesn't mean true as in nonfiction. He means true as in true to an idea. True to its theme. There's an audience out there for every true idea.

What it means to you:

_____

_____

_____

_____

_____

245.

"The writer must write what he has to say, not speak it."
—Ernest Hemingway

My take:

Unlike casual conversation, writing requires precision, thoughtfulness, and artistry.

What it means to you:

_____

_____

_____

_____

_____

246.

"There is no greater joy than the joy of beginning."
—Cesare Pavese

My take:

Finishing a project is pretty joyful too, but there's something about starting one with all of its many possibilities that excites the mind and heart.

What it means to you:

_____
_____
_____
_____
_____
_____

247.

"The end of a story should be a door left slightly ajar."
—Alan Bennett

My take:

Always leave the reader with a little something to ponder.

What it means to you:

_____
_____
_____
_____
_____
_____

248.

"The one thing that you have that nobody else has is you. Your voice, your mind, your story, your vision."

—Neil Gaiman

My take:

What separates you from all the other writers? You! Lean into it.

What it means to you:

_____

_____

_____

_____

_____

249.

"The role of a writer is to create the reader."
–Jorge Luis Borges

My take:

It's up to you to make the person who picks up your book more than just someone who picks up your book.

What it means to you:

_____

_____

_____

_____

_____

250.

"When you write, you write not to be read but to be heard."
–James Baldwin

My take:

There's a difference. Being heard means getting through.

What it means to you:

_____

_____

_____

_____

_____

251.

"The reader completes the story."
—Terry Tempest Williams

My take:

Writer and reader: a collaborative effort. Never completely button everything up. Leave some room to engage the reader's imagination.

What it means to you:

_____

_____

_____

_____

_____

252.

> "What I like in a good author is not what they say, but what they whisper."
>
> —Logan Pearsall Smith

My take:

A plea for subtlety. There's a difference between getting your thoughts across and beating the reader over the head. Learn the difference and you'll be a much more effective writer.

What it means to you:

_____

_____

_____

_____

_____

253.

"Good stories teach us how to live; great ones teach us how to change the world."

—Jacqueline Woodson

My take:

A noble quest. But not all of us can be world-changers. If you can impart some lessons on how to live, celebrate that.

What it means to you:

_____

_____

_____

_____

_____

_____

254.

"A writer must leave room for the reader to bring themselves into the story."

—Margaret Atwood

My take:

Another admonition to stop beating things so hard. You'll never get a reader engaged by doing all the work for them.

What it means to you:

_____

_____

_____

_____

_____

255.

"Every reader brings their own history to a book, and so every reading is unique."
—Alice Hoffman

My take:

And so don't be surprised if a reader gets something out of your work that you never even intended. But that's a good thing.

What it means to you:

_____

_____

_____

_____

_____

_____

256.

"Writers have the ability to plant seeds of empathy in the hearts of readers."

—Chimamanda Ngozi Adichie

My take:

You can make a reader feel something for a character they never would have thought possible, if you do it right.

What it means to you:

_____

_____

_____

_____

_____

257.

"Stories can heal what the world breaks."
–Jesmyn Ward

My take:

Words as medicine? You bet.

What it means to you:

_____

_____

_____

_____

_____

258.

"When the story is good enough, it will tell you how it wants to be written."

—Gabriel García Márquez

My take:

It's amazing when this happens. The path forward becomes crystal clear.

What it means to you:

_____

_____

_____

_____

_____

259.

"When you write, you lay out a line of words. The line of words is a miner's pick, a woodcarver's gouge, a surgeon's probe."

—Annie Dillard

My take:

And each line takes you deeper, uncovering the story within. It's down there somewhere. Keep digging.

What it means to you:

_____

_____

_____

_____

_____

_____

260.

"Find your own voice, and then let it sing."
—Madeleine L'Engle

My take:

And sing loudly. You've got your own unique voice and you mustn't hide it. Let the world hear you!

What it means to you:

_____

_____

_____

_____

_____

_____

261.

"Style is not how you write. It is how you do not write like anyone else."

—Charles Ghigna

My take:

If you're copying someone else's style, you're not offering your prospective reader anything new.

What it means to you:

_____

_____

_____

_____

_____

_____

262.

"The best time to begin writing is yesterday."
—Elizabeth George

My take:

But since yesterday is gone, you'd better get started today.

What it means to you:

_____

_____

_____

_____

_____

263.

"Write about what disturbs you, particularly if it bothers no one else."
—Kathryn Stockett

My take:

If somebody's not disturbed by what disturbs you, it's probably because nobody has presented it properly to them yet. That's where you come in.

What it means to you:

264.

"The writer is an observer of life and a translator for the world."

—Elizabeth Hardwick

My take:

Life has so much to tell us. It's the writer that puts it all into words for others to better comprehend.

What it means to you:

_____

_____

_____

_____

_____

_____

265.

"The reader has to see themselves in the work; otherwise, the words remain lifeless."

–Jhumpa Lahiri

My take:

Writing comes to life only when we can relate to it. If it doesn't resonate with us somehow, it loses us.

What it means to you:

_____

_____

_____

_____

_____

_____

266.

"The writer owes the reader honesty, even in fiction."
—Michael Cunningham

My take:

All writing has to ring with truth. Even fiction needs to be sincere and genuine and true to its theme.

What it means to you:

_____

_____

_____

_____

_____

_____

267.

"Your audience is not just a demographic. It is the collective heartbeat of those who need your words."

—Janice Hardy

My take:

You'll have plenty of time to figure out how to market your book to the people most likely to buy it. That should never be a concern as you're writing.

What it means to you:

_____

_____

_____

_____

_____

268.

"What a miracle it is that out of these small, flat, rigid squares of paper unfolds world after world after world."

—Anne Lamott

My take:

You know, it really is a miracle. Never take what you're doing for granted. It is nothing less than amazing.

What it means to you:

_____

_____

_____

_____

_____

269.

"Stories aren't made of language: they're made of something else... perhaps they're made of life."
—Philip Pullman

My take:

Stories are so much more than words.

What it means to you:

_____

_____

_____

_____

_____

270.

"There is no greater power on this earth than story."
—Libba Bray

My take:

Nothing moves people more. Nothing touches them more. Nothing inspires them more.

What it means to you:

_____

_____

_____

_____

_____

271.

"You may tell a tale that takes up residence in someone's soul, becomes their blood and self, and purpose. That is your role, your gift."

—Erin Morgenstern

My take:

Big responsibility, isn't it? Not to be taken lightly.

What it means to you:

_____

_____

_____

_____

_____

272.

"Lock up your libraries if you like; but there is no gate, no lock, no bolt that you can set upon the freedom of my mind."
—Virginia Woolf

My take:
Which is why writing will never die.

What it means to you:

_____

_____

_____

_____

_____

_____

273.

"If you are not afraid of the voices inside you, you will not fear the critics outside you."
—Natalie Goldberg

My take:

I have always found those interior voices to be the most intimidating. The ones that tell you that you can't do it. That you're no good. Learn to handle them and you'll be just fine.

What it means to you:

_____

_____

_____

_____

_____

_____

274.

"Examine every word you put on paper. You'll find a surprising number that don't serve any purpose."
—William Zinsser

My take:

If you've ever read anything that dragged and was totally lacking in flow, it's a good bet it was leaden with unnecessary words.

What it means to you:

_____
_____
_____
_____
_____

275.

"The impulse to write things down is a peculiarly compulsive one, inexplicable to those who do not share it."

–Joan Didion

My take:

Do you have people in your life that scratch their heads at your apparent need to write everything down? You're not alone!

What it means to you:

_____

_____

_____

_____

_____

276.

"A sentence should contain no unnecessary words, a paragraph no unnecessary sentences, for the same reason a machine should have no unnecessary parts."

— William Strunk Jr. and E. B. White

My take:

Streamline! Be efficient. Machine-like. (Only with heart.)

What it means to you:

_____

_____

_____

_____

_____

277.

"Atticus told me to delete the adjectives and I'd have the facts."

— Harper Lee

My take:

Talk about listening to the story! Harper Lee took advice from a character. (Good advice, and something I can imagine Atticus Finch passing along.)

What it means to you:

_____

_____

_____

_____

_____

278.

"A great novel, rather than discouraging me, simply makes me want to write."
—Madeleine L'Engle

My take:

Yes, don't be intimidated by great writing! Let it inspire you instead.

What it means to you:

_____

_____

_____

_____

_____

279.

"I read and feel that same compulsion; the desire to possess what [the writer] has written, which can only be subdued by writing something myself."

—Patti Smith

My take:

Good writing does this, doesn't it? It makes you want to write.

What it means to you:

_____

_____

_____

_____

_____

280.

"The only way to learn to write is to force yourself to produce a certain number of words on a regular basis."

—William Zinsser

My take:

I think this is good, practical advice. But not just for learning to write, but also for your day-to-day routine. I try for 1,000 words per day. Find what works best for you.

What it means to you:

_____

_____

_____

_____

_____

281.

"Prose is architecture, not interior decoration."
—Ernest Hemingway

My take:

Hemingway was famous for simplicity and function. No fancy embellishments and unnecessary adornments.

What it means to you:

_____

_____

_____

_____

_____

282.

"This is the only real concern of the artist, to recreate out of the disorder of life that order which is art."

—James Baldwin

My take:

Writers make sense of life. And that *is art.*

What it means to you:

_____

_____

_____

_____

_____

283.

"A storyteller makes up things to help other people; a liar makes up things to help himself."

—Daniel Wallace

My take:

I knew there was a difference!

What it means to you:

_____

_____

_____

_____

_____

_____

284.

"Your style is your fingerprint. Don't try to imitate someone else's."
—Pablo Neruda

My take:

Just be you. After all, every other writer is already taken.

What it means to you:

_____

_____

_____

_____

_____

_____

285.

"A writer's life and work are not a gift to mankind; they are its necessity."
—Toni Morrison

My take:

Hear that? We're needed.

What it means to you:

_____

_____

_____

_____

_____

_____

286.

"We are cups, quietly and constantly being filled. The trick is knowing how to tip ourselves over and let the beautiful stuff out."

—Ray Bradbury

My take:

Everything you experience is fodder for that next wonderful piece of writing that you can share with the world.

What it means to you:

_____

_____

_____

_____

_____

287.

"Everything that needs to be said has already been said. But, since no one was listening, everything must be said again."

—André Gide

My take:

And it's your job to say it in a different way. Maybe this time they'll hear it.

What it means to you:

_____

_____

_____

_____

_____

288.

"Sometimes I write better than I can."
—Ernest Hemingway

My take:

You never know when you're going to surprise yourself. Maybe you've mentally put an upper limit on your skill level that really isn't there.

What it means to you:

_____

_____

_____

_____

_____

289.

"You can't blame the author for what the characters say."
—Truman Capote

My take:

Characters have lives of their own. You're just reporting on those lives.

What it means to you:

_____

_____

_____

_____

_____

_____

290.

"A writer is someone who has taught his mind to misbehave."
— Oscar Wilde

My take:

Because creativity means painting outside the proverbial lines.

What it means to you:

_____

_____

_____

_____

_____

291.

"You know what I did after I wrote my first novel? I shut up and wrote twenty-three more."
—Michael Connelly

My take:

You're not doing this just to get published one time, right? You're doing this because you love to write. So keep writing!

What it means to you:

_____

_____

_____

_____

_____

_____

292.

"We surrender the outcomes because we cannot control how people are going to respond to us and our work in the world."

—Rob Bell

My take:

This surrending idea is terribly hard to master. But the truth is, once your writing is out there, you have no control over how it will be received, and you have to let it go.

What it means to you:

_____

_____

_____

_____

_____

293.

"Mistakes are the portals of discovery."
–James Joyce

My take:

And that's why you shouldn't be afraid to make mistakes.

What it means to you:

_____

_____

_____

_____

_____

294.

"The time to begin writing an article is when you have finished it to your satisfaction."
—Mark Twain

My take:

Ha! Because that's when you really have it all thought out. Yep, that would be a good time to start writing it (again).

What it means to you:

_____

_____

_____

_____

_____

295.

"Be ruthless about protecting writing days."
—J.K. Rowling

My take:

Don't let anyone hijack your time. If you work at home like I do and set your own hours, you're probably experienced with the idea that people think you're somehow always available. Three words: "Sorry, I'm writing."

What it means to you:

_____

_____

_____

_____

_____

296.

"A writer is a writer because, even when there is no hope, even when nothing you do shows any sign of promise, you keep writing anyway."

— Junot Diaz

My take:

As good a definition as there is.

What it means to you:

_____
_____
_____
_____
_____

297.

"Write quickly and you will never write well; write well, and you will soon write quickly."

—Marcus Fabius Quintilianus

My take:

I know from experience that this is true. You get better, and it becomes easier. And easier means faster.

What it means to you:

_____

_____

_____

_____

_____

298.

"A good story is a dream shared by the author and the reader. Anything that wakes the reader from the dream is a mortal sin."

—Victor J. Banis

My take:

This is another way of saying that you have to make your readers forget they're reading words. Give them an experience.

What it means to you:

_____

_____

_____

_____

_____

299.

"Don't use adjectives which merely tell us how you want us to feel about the thing you are describing. Describe it. The adjectives are only like saying to your readers, 'Please will you do my job for me.'"

— C.S. Lewis

My take:

If it's sad, describe it so that the reader will conclude, for themselves: *"That's sad."*

What it means to you:

_____

_____

_____

_____

_____

300.

"Good writing is supposed to evoke sensation in the reader – not the fact that it is raining, but the feeling of being rained upon."

—E. L. Doctorow

My take:

Show, don't tell!

What it means to you:

_____

_____

_____

_____

_____

301.

"All good writing leaves something unexpressed."
—Christian Nestell Bovee

My take:

Always leave something for the reader to mull over. If you can keep them engaged, even after they've finished reading—well, that's like hitting the jackpot.

What it means to you:

_____

_____

_____

_____

_____

_____

302.

"You do an awful lot of bad writing in order to do any good writing. It would be very interesting to make a collection of some of the worst writing by good writers."

—William S. Burroughs

My take:

I love this idea. Wouldn't you like to read the very first drafts of some of the real classics? Bet they weren't very good.

What it means to you:

_____

_____

_____

_____

_____

_____

303.

"A good novel tells us the truth about its hero; but a bad novel tells us the truth about its author."

—G.K. Chesterton

My take:

And he doesn't just mean that the truth is that author is a bad writer. He means that the novel is bad because it's self-indulgent.

What it means to you:

_____

_____

_____

_____

_____

304.

"The secret of being a bore is to tell everything."
—Voltaire

My take:

Intrigue often comes from what's left unsaid.

What it means to you:

_____
_____
_____
_____
_____

305.

"It's not wise to violate the rules until you know how to observe them."
–T.S. Eliot

My take:

Great point. We talk about breaking the rules as writers, but maybe we need to learn how to master them before we set about breaching them.

What it means to you:

_____

_____

_____

_____

_____

306.

"Plot is no more than footprints left in the snow after your characters have run by on their way to incredible destinations."

—Ray Bradbury

My take:

Great novels have great characters. The plot is a vehicle by which to showcase them.

What it means to you:

_____

_____

_____

_____

_____

307.

"What I've learned about writing is that sometimes less is more, while often more is grander. And both are true."
—Richelle E. Goodrich

My take:

Depends on the project, right? Each has its own requirements.

What it means to you:

_____

_____

_____

_____

_____

308.

"I've found the best way to revise your own work is to pretend that somebody else wrote it and then to rip the living shit out of it."

—Don Roff

My take:

Ha! True. Objectivity is the name of the game.

What it means to you:

_____

_____

_____

_____

_____

309.

"Put down everything that comes into your head and then you're a writer. But an author is one who can judge his own stuff's worth, without pity, and destroy most of it."

—Colette

My take:

The difference between writer and author. Interesting.

What it means to you:

_____

_____

_____

_____

_____

310.

"I have only made this letter longer because I have not had the time to make it shorter."

—Blaise Pascal

My take:

Right? It takes time and effort to write smartly and concisely. It's a lot faster to just ramble.

What it means to you:

_____

_____

_____

_____

_____

311.

"Write like you're a goddamn death row inmate and the governor is out of the country and there's no chance for a pardon."
—Alan Watts

My take:

That ought to give you a sense of urgency!

What it means to you:

_____

_____

_____

_____

_____

312.

"One should use common words to say uncommon things."

—Arthur Schopenhauer

My take:

Your ideas might be unique and fascinating, but if they're not understandable, or if they're otherwise poorly written, nobody will care what they are.

What it means to you:

_____

_____

_____

_____

_____

313.

"He asked, 'What makes a man a writer?' 'Well,' I said, 'it's simple. You either get it down on paper, or jump off a bridge.'"

—Charles Bukowski

My take:

When you're driven to write…

What it means to you:

_____

_____

_____

_____

_____

_____

314.

"How vain it is to sit down to write when you have not stood up to live."

—Henry David Thoreau

My take:

If you have not tasted life, how can you expect to write about it?

What it means to you:

_____

_____

_____

_____

_____

315.

"Work like hell! I had 122 rejection slips before I sold a story."

—F. Scott Fitzgerald

My take:

Makes you wonder if, today, Fitzgerald would have just dispensed with all that and self-published.

What it means to you:

_____

_____

_____

_____

_____

_____

316.

"In displaying the psychology of your characters, minute particulars are essential. God save us from vague generalizations!"

—Anton Chekhov

My take:

Flesh those characters out. Make them real.

What it means to you:

_____
_____
_____
_____
_____

317.

"Storytelling is as natural as breathing; plotting is the literary version of artificial respiration."

—Stephen King

My take:

Don't control your story so tightly. Allow the story room to breathe.

What it means to you:

_____

_____

_____

_____

_____

318.

"It unfolds as you write it. That's something I never believed before I wrote a book, but it does."

—Joan Didion

My take:

Something to keep in mind when you think you're stuck or can't even get started. Just write. The book will soon present itself.

What it means to you:

_____

_____

_____

_____

_____

319.

"Address the people you seek, and them only."
—Claude C. Hopkins

My take:

Your writing can't be all things to all people. Nor should you try to make it so.

What it means to you:

_____

_____

_____

_____

_____

_____

320.

"The cure for boredom is curiosity. There is no cure for curiosity."

—Dorothy Parker

My take:

And that's a good thing. All great writers are curious.

What it means to you:

_____

_____

_____

_____

_____

_____

321.

"Books choose their authors; the act of creation is not entirely a rational and conscious one."
—Salman Rushdie

My take:

It really isn't. Most of the time, you just feel inepxlicably drawn to a certain idea or theme to explore and write about.

What it means to you:

_____

_____

_____

_____

_____

322.

"If you only read the books that everyone else is reading, you can only think what everyone else is thinking."
—Haruki Murakami

My take:

Great piece of advice. Search out the obscure.

What it means to you:

_____

_____

_____

_____

_____

_____

323.

"A year from now you may wish you had started today."
—Karen Lamb

My take:

So stop procrastinating. Put another way, if you had started your book a year ago, you might be finished now.

What it means to you:

_____

_____

_____

_____

_____

324.

"Don't bother just to be better than your contemporaries or predecessors. Try to be better than yourself."
—William Faulkner

My take:

It's so easy to try to compare yourself with other writers. Waste of time. Just keep improving.

What it means to you:

_____

_____

_____

_____

_____

325.

"The freelance writer is a man who is paid per piece or per word or perhaps."

—Robert Benchley

My take:

Oh, don't I know the truth of this one!

What it means to you:

_____

_____

_____

_____

_____

326.

"Either write something worth reading or do something worth writing."
—Benjamin Franklin

My take:

Yep, those are the choices.

What it means to you:

_____
_____
_____
_____
_____

327.

"As a writer, you should not judge, you should understand."

—Ernest Hemingway

My take:

Judging your characters can come across as if you have an agenda. Seek instead to understand why they do what they do.

What it means to you:

_____

_____

_____

_____

_____

328.

"I would advise anyone who aspires to a writing career that before developing his talent he would be wise to develop a thick hide."

—Harper Lee

My take:

You will get bad reviews, and even if they're just 1-star reviews from strangers on Amazon, they're going to sting a bit.

What it means to you:

_____

_____

_____

_____

_____

_____

329.

"It's better to be done than for it to be done perfectly."
—Amy Collins

My take:

Because it will never be done if it's to be done perfectly. There's no such thing. So if you're holding out for that, you're going to be holding out for a long time.

What it means to you:

_____

_____

_____

_____

_____

330.

"Let anything happen! Be messy! Be wild!"
—Windy Lynn Harris

My take:

All part of the creative process. Lean into it.

What it means to you:

_____

_____

_____

_____

_____

331.

"There is just one rule: Keep your readers reading."
—Paula Munier

My take:

There are quotes in here about writing having no rules but you know what? This one seems like a pretty good one.

What it means to you:

_____

_____

_____

_____

_____

332.

"Two voices battle for control in every writer's head: Your internal editor is on your side, making you better. Your internal critic is against you and needs to be quieted."

—Jane Cleland

My take:

That internal critic can be awfully loud. Tell 'em to get bent.

What it means to you:

_____

_____

_____

_____

_____

_____

333.

"Showing someone your writing is kind of like taking off your clothes."
–Min Jin Lee

My take:

Oh, that feeling of vulnerability. You're not alone. We all feel it.

What it means to you:

_____

_____

_____

_____

_____

334.

"I think the job of writing and literature is to encourage each one of us to believe that we're living in a story."

—Naomi Shihab Nye

My take:

Because art imitates life.

What it means to you:

_____
_____
_____
_____
_____

335.

"Everybody is talented because everybody who is human has something to express."
—Brenda Ueland

My take:
And not just something. Something of value.

What it means to you:

_____

_____

_____

_____

_____

336.

"Let me live, love, and say it well in good sentences."
—Sylvia Plath

My take:

What more can a writer ask?

What it means to you:

_____

_____

_____

_____

_____

337.

"Exercise the writing muscle every day, even if it is only a letter, notes, a title list, a character sketch, a journal entry. Writers are like dancers, like athletes. Without that exercise, the muscles seize up."

—Jane Yolen

My take:

Don't get rusty. What have you written today?

What it means to you:

_____

_____

_____

_____

_____

_____

338.

"It is with words as with sunbeams - the more they are condensed, the deeper they burn."

—Robert Southey

My take:

Concision is power.

What it means to you:

_____

_____

_____

_____

_____

_____

339.

"The whole labor of writing is to make it look like it just came off the top of your head."
—Paddy Chayefsky

My take:

Great writing flows so well and looks so simple that it's hard to imagine the toil that went into it. But the toil is why it flows so well and looks so simple.

What it means to you:

_____

_____

_____

_____

_____

340.

"The art of writing has for backbone some fierce attachment to an idea"
—Virginia Woolf

My take:

An essay or article or novel—any piece of writing—has to be about something.

What it means to you:

_____

_____

_____

_____

_____

_____

341.

"I rewrote the ending of Farewell to Arms *39 times* before I was satisfied."
—Ernest Hemingway

My take:

And he got it perfect. That's how important rewriting is.

What it means to you:

_____

_____

_____

_____

_____

342.

"The craft or art of writing is the clumsy attempt to find symbols for the wordlessness."
—John Steinbeck

My take:

That's what we writers do. Translate life.

What it means to you:

_____

_____

_____

_____

_____

343.

"The art of writing fiction is to sail as dangerously close to the truth as possible without sinking the ship."

—Kinky Friedman

My take:

Great fiction reflects the real. It's fiction, but it's truth.

What it means to you:

_____

_____

_____

_____

_____

_____

344.

"I love writing. I love the swirl and swing of words as they tangle with human emotions."

—James Michener

My take:

Yes, the power of language, the way words can interact to produce something meaningful. That's writing.

What it means to you:

_____

_____

_____

_____

_____

345.

"That's the thing about books, they let you travel without moving your feet."
—Jhumpa Lahiri

My take:

Books can take you to other worlds, and let you see life from other perspectives.

What it means to you:

_____

_____

_____

_____

_____

_____

346.

"And now that you don't have to be perfect, you can be good."

— John Steinbeck

My take:

Another admonition to forget about perfection. How liberating!

What it means to you:

_____

_____

_____

_____

_____

_____

347.

"No need to force yourself to do something the 'right way' if it's not your right way. Your job is to honor your process."
—Andi Cumbo

My take:

In fact, there is no "right" way. There's only your way.

What it means to you:

_____

_____

_____

_____

_____

348.

"When I write, I give people access to their own emotions."
—Gord Downie

My take:

Reading something powerful often moves us toward introspection in a way we might otherwise never have moved.

What it means to you:

_____

_____

_____

_____

_____

349.

> "The idea is to write it so that people hear it and it slides through the brain and goes straight to the heart."
>
> —Maya Angelou

My take:

*Reaching people intellectually is all well and good, but if you can reach them emotionally, then you've **really** reached them.*

What it means to you:

_____

_____

_____

_____

_____

350.

"There is something delicious about writing the first words of a story. You never quite know where they'll take you."

—Beatrix Potter

My take:

It really is exciting. Oh, the possibilities!

What it means to you:

_____

_____

_____

_____

_____

351.

"If something inside of you is real, we will probably find it interesting, and it will probably be universal. So you must risk placing real emotion at the center of your work."

—Anne Lamott

My take:

If you feel it, others feel it, too. So don't be afraid to share it. That's how great writing connects.

What it means to you:

_____

_____

_____

_____

_____

352.

"It's a bizarre but wonderful feeling to arrive dead center of a target you didn't even know you were aiming for."

—Lois McMaster Bujold

My take:

This happens all the time, thus highlighting the importance of being flexible with what it is you're writing.

What it means to you:

_____

_____

_____

_____

_____

_____

353.

"Anyone who says writing is easy isn't doing it right."
—Amy Joy

My take:

We know that, don't we? Good writing is hard work. (Conversely, bad writing can be very easy.)

What it means to you:

_____

_____

_____

_____

_____

354.

"Quantity produces quality. If you only write a few things, you're doomed."
—Ray Bradbury

My take:

And not everything you write is going to be any good. But you'll become much better by writing more and more.

What it means to you:

_____

_____

_____

_____

_____

_____

355.

"Having someone who believes in you makes a lot of difference. They don't have to make speeches. Just believing is usually enough."

—Stephen King

My take:

Boy, this is important. Everybody needs a supporter. Hope you have someone in your life who believes.

What it means to you:

_____

_____

_____

_____

_____

356.

"Real seriousness in regard to writing is one of the two absolute necessities. The other, unfortunately, is talent."

—Ernest Hemingway

My take:

Well, yes, you really can't get around it. If you don't have the talent...

What it means to you:

_____

_____

_____

_____

_____

_____

357.

"My family can always tell when I'm well into a novel because the meals get very crummy."

—Anne Tyler

My take:

Ha! Priorities, priorities!

What it means to you:

_____

_____

_____

_____

_____

358.

"Everybody walks past a thousand story ideas every day. The good writers are the ones who see five or six of them. Most people don't see any."

—Orson Scott Card

My take:

Good writers are great observers.

What it means to you:

_____

_____

_____

_____

_____

359.

"There comes a point in your life when you need to stop reading other people's books and write your own."

—Albert Einstein

My take:

Are you there yet?

What it means to you:

_____

_____

_____

_____

_____

360.

"Good fiction's job is to comfort the disturbed and disturb the comfortable"
—David Foster Wallace

My take:

Yep, duel purposes, all depending on the reader's state of mind.

What it means to you:

_____

_____

_____

_____

_____

361.

"The writer's greatest gift is the ability to create a world that never existed before."
—Arthur Conan Doyle

My take:

That's what we do. Create worlds. How cool is that?

What it means to you:

_____

_____

_____

_____

_____

362.

"A book is never a masterpiece: it becomes one. Genius is the talent of a dead man."

—Maxwell Perkins

My take:

The editor of such greats as Hemingway and Fitzgerald was saying that very little greatness gets recognized in its time. Will people still be reading and talking about it a hundred years from now? That's true genius.

What it means to you:

_____

_____

_____

_____

_____

363.

"The key to all story endings is to give the audience what it wants, but not in the way it expects."

—William Goldman

My take:

Satisfy them, but don't be predictable.

What it means to you:

_____

_____

_____

_____

_____

364.

"Focus more on your desire than on your doubt, and the dream will take care of itself."
—Mark Twain

My take:

Desire always trumps fear. Doubt is no match for enthusiasm.

What it means to you:

_____

_____

_____

_____

_____

365.

"I asked how can you ever be sure that what you write is really any good at all and he said you can't...you can never be sure...you die without knowing whether anything you wrote was any good...if you have to be sure don't write."

—W.S. Merwin

My take:

From a poem Merwin wrote about the poet John Berryman. And I have nothing more to add!

What it means to you:

_____

_____

_____

_____

_____

About the Author

Jerry Payne is an award-winning ghostwriter of over forty books and author of *Writing Memoir: The Practical Guide to Writing and Publishing the Story of Your Life*. More recently, he has taken his life-long interest in the deeper questions of the universe and written, under the pen name "G.S. Payne," *So Who is God, Anyway?: An Unorthodox Theory for Doubters, Skeptics, and Recovering Fundamentalists*. Both these works can be found on Amazon and wherever books are sold.

Payne lives in upstate South Carolina and when he's not writing or mulling the big questions, he can be found on Lake Hartwell sailing his sloop *Pilar*, named after Ernest Hemingway's fishing boat. He also enjoys the cinema and traveling, and when engaged in the latter, he seeks out historic hotels (preferably haunted ones) and good Irish pubs. Of all the things he's most proud of, being a father and grandfather top the list.

www.ingramcontent.com/pod-product-compliance
Lightning Source LLC
Chambersburg PA
CBHW020531030426
42337CB00013B/804